Accidentally Vegan

Italian Soups

Many people contributed to this work including Rita Arra, Rachele Puntel, Nancy Soper, Mia Caruso, Shannon Parker, Giovanna Buda, and Sofia Caruso.

Copyright © 2020, Judgmental Owl Press

Photography © 2020, Giovanni Caruso

This book may not be reproduced in whole or in part by any means (with the exception of short quotes for the purpose of review) without the permission of the publisher. For more information on our books email **veganitalian@outlook.com** or write: Judgmental Owl Press, 2411 South 8th Street West, Missoula, MT 59801

Created, designed, and published in the USA.

ISBN: 979-8-64-930897-7

Accidentally Vegan

Italian Soups

Simple versions of 30 forgotten Italian soups that always were and always will be vegan

Giovanni Caruso

To my nephew Nick, who first told me about The China Study, and my niece Ila, whose good natured but remorselessly critical review of an early draft caused me to produce a book that is as good as I could make it.

CONTENTS

INTRODUCTION 1
Soffritto 2
Vegetable Stock 3
Bread 4
Beans 5
Garnishes 5
Recipes as Suggestions 6
Organization of the Book 7

FACILISSIMO (VERY EASY) 9
Zuppa di Pomodori e Finocchi (Tomato and Fennel Soup) 10
Crema di Cannellini alla Paprika (Cannellini Bean Soup with Paprika) 12
Zuppa di Patate, Porri, e Funghi (Potato, Leek, and Mushroom Soup) 14
Zuppa Autunnale (Autumn Soup) 16
Minestrone di Orzo e Legumi (Barley and Legume Soup) 18
Zuppa di Lenticchie Rosse (Red Lentil Soup) 20
Zuppa di Carciofi e Funghi (Artichoke and Mushroom Soup) 22
Vellutata di Spinaci e Pistacchi (Spinach and Pistachio Soup) 24
Vellutata di Porri e Patate (Cream of Leek and Potato Soup) 26
Pappa al Pomodoro (Tomato and Bread Soup) 28
Crema di Porcini e Castagne (Mushroom and Chestnut Soup) 30
Zuppa di Cipolle (Onion Soup) 32

FACILE (EASY) 35
Zuppa di Piselli Spezzati (Split Pea Soup) 36
Zuppa di Zucca e Ceci (Pumpkin and Chickpea Soup) 38
Zuppa di Fagioli Bianchi (Tuscan White Bean Soup) 40
Pasta e Ceci (Pasta and Chickpea Soup) 42
Minestra di Lenticchie e Scarola (Lentil and Escarole Soup) 44
Crema di Asparagi e Patate (Cream of Asparagus and Potato Soup) 46
Crema di Broccoli al Limone (Cream of Broccoli Soup) 48
Bordatino Pisano (On Board Soup) 50
Zuppa del Contadino (Farmer's Soup) 52
Maccú di San Giuseppe (Saint Joseph's Soup) 54
Zuppa di Zucca e Castagne (Pumpkin and Chestnut Soup) 56
Zuppa di Legumi e Erbe Aromatiche (Legume and Herb Soup) 58
Sbroscia (Table Scrap Soup) 60
Zuppa d'Inverno (Winter Soup) 62

UN PO' PIÚ DIFFICILE (A BIT MORE DIFFICULT) 65
Maccú (Fava Bean Soup) 66
Ciambotta (Vegetable Stew) 68
Ribollita (Reboiled Soup) 70
Crema di Fave e Asparagi (Cream of Fava and Asparagus Soup) 72

INTRODUCTION

Individuals interested in vegan Italian cooking are often led to meat and dairy substitutions. Dishes such as spaghetti and beetballs and the use of cheese and meat substitutes made from nuts or soybeans abound. Or, the suggestion is made to simply remove an ingredient or two to create vegan versions of Italian dishes, but at some cost to the integrity of the original dish, to be sure. Although these are valid approaches to cooking Italian food in a vegan manner, my tactic is to select traditional and authentic Italian dishes that are vegan not through substitution or omission, but by their very nature. From *sbroscia* and *bordatino pisano* to *maccú* and *pappa al pomodoro*, the vegan soups in this book are not widely known outside of Italy, but they should be.

Throughout the history of the peninsula, the Italian diet has been largely vegetarian and often vegan, particularly in the South. Farmers and cooks in Southern Italy learned centuries ago that to survive in this mountainous, often hot and challenging location required efficiencies in food production which necessitated growing and subsisting largely on vegetables, both fresh and preserved, rather than on meat or dairy products. It was not economically feasible to maintain a cow just for milk production to make butter when olives to make olive oil were so readily available and suited to the land and climate. It was not economically feasible to provide large stock animals with the tremendous amount of water and grazing land they require when a fraction of those resources could be used to grow a plethora of delicious vegetables. This is why so many traditional Italian dishes had little or no meat or dairy products. We are re-learning these lessons today as levels of consciousness about the ethical and environmental implications of what we eat are rising. This book was written to help those desiring to maintain a vegan diet to have ready access to completely traditional (no beetballs here), delicious, economical, rustic, and healthy Italian food.

The soups in this cookbook are not difficult to prepare. Through years of selfless testing and tasting (you're welcome), I have created simple versions of traditional Italian soups that have, for the most part, been forgotten outside of Italy or were never introduced outside her borders. After the French "borrowed" Italian cuisine during the Renaissance, they created overly complicated and derivative versions of Italian dishes in which the flavors and simplicity were sacrificed, and they somehow convinced the world that this was classical cuisine. In this book, we return to authentic Italian cuisine with a focus on strong flavors, simple preparations, and hearty soups that allow the ingredients to be enjoyed as nature intended. The remainder of this introduction contains a discussion of several key concerns when cooking accidentally vegan Italian soups.

SOFFRITTO

If there is one thing that makes or breaks an Italian soup it is the *soffritto*. The soffritto is the gently fried aromatic vegetables that begin the process of flavor development in Italian sauces and soups. The soffritto is what makes a dish taste like it has been gently bubbling away in an old cast iron pot over an open flame for hours. Usually, this consists of carrots, celery, and onions, finely diced, and fried in plenty of olive oil with a pinch of salt. The salt helps draw out the water in the vegetables and this facilitates the cooking process. Often other ingredients are substituted or added such as leeks, crushed red pepper, dried or fresh herbs, garlic, and tomato or tomato paste. Regarding the olive oil used for the soffritto, I feel that I should apologize to Americans for how *much* olive oil is recommended in the recipes in this book, and as well to Italians for how *little*. One of the benefits of enjoying vegan meals is that without all the saturated fat, cholesterol, and calories found in many non-vegan dishes, we can easily afford an extra tablespoon or two of delicious olive oil.

The ingredients for the soffritto are prepared *tritato*, meaning that they are cut into relatively small sizes prior to cooking (about ¼ inch or ½ centimeter). Larger pieces result in longer cooking times and uneven cooking. Using a food processor is the quickest and easiest way to achieve *un bel tritato* (a beautiful dice). If the standard carrot, celery, and onion soffritto is called for, placing the carrots at the bottom of the food processor with the celery and onions on top keeps the celery and onion from liquifying. I find that pulsing the machine about ten times for a couple of seconds each, giving a stir, and pulsing again three or four times usually works well. If you do not have a food processor, it is a simple matter to dice the vegetables by hand, but it is important to produce small pieces.

The word soffritto literally means under fried, or softly fried, and this refers to the cooking temperature. We are not *French!* (Well, maybe some of us are, but not at the moment). We do not *sauté* our aromatics (*mirepoix*) at a high temperature, scarring them, scaring them, burning some parts while leaving others raw, incinerating them into submission. When using this cookbook, we are Italians, and we gently coax and tempt and tease our aromatics into releasing their best flavors. On my gas range, I find that halfway between 3 and 4 on the 1 through 10 scale works well. When I return to the stove to check on my soffritto, I like to see the vegetables relaxing in a bubbling jacuzzi of olive oil, happily reaching their well-deserved culinary potential after a long season of tireless photosynthesizing, poor dears. The soffritto should appear wet, so if it looks dry add an extra drizzle of olive oil.

In this book, some of the recipes call for a light soffritto, meaning that the ingredients are gently fried for about 5 minutes so that no significant coloring occurs (although some translucence for the onions will be achieved). Others call for a dark soffritto, meaning that the ingredients are gently fried for 15 minutes or more, with the goal being to create substantial caramelization of the sugars in the vegetables. In between, and most commonly, we have a golden soffritto, what the Italians would call *soffritto dorato*, which results from gently frying the vegetables for about 10-15 minutes depending on the type and amount of ingredients. The type of soffritto recommended for each recipe will be specified in the procedures, but the cooking time can vary a bit based on your particular stove settings and the size and type of ingredients.

VEGETABLE STOCK

If there is a second crucial component to making great Italian soups, it is the *brodo vegetale*, or vegetable stock (In English, *broth* usually refers to something to be eaten, whereas *stock* refers to something to be used as an ingredient, the latter applying in our case). Although water can be used as the liquid base for some soups, the use of a nutritious and delicious homemade vegetable stock is an opportunity to add complexity and depth to the soup's flavors. Homemade vegetable stock is not only easy to make, it's *free*. That's right, I'm about to tell you the secret to a lifetime's supply of free homemade vegetable stock. When you chop or clean vegetables such as carrots, onions (especially onions!), broccoli, asparagus, leeks (especially leeks!), cauliflower, tomatoes, garlic, parsley stems, and mushrooms (especially mushrooms!), put the skins, stalks, tops, and bottoms in the freezer. If you have vegetables in the refrigerator that are a bit past their prime (not moldy), throw them in the freezer rather than the trash.

Then, when you need vegetable stock, simply simmer some of these odds and ends in water for about an hour and remove the vegetable pieces. It is best not to use starchy vegetables such as potatoes or sweet potatoes because they make the stock cloudy. The brown papery outside skin of onions gives the stock a beautiful color, although adding purple cabbage, beets, or red/purple onion skins gives the predictably colorful result which may not be desired. A single container can be used for all the various items in the freezer, and they will keep for a year. After you make the stock, it keeps nicely in the refrigerator for five days, so you can make enough for two batches of soup. Not only is this easy, but by saving your scraps rather than buying commercial stocks, you are lessening your environmental impact and padding your checking account while enjoying stock that is dramatically better and healthier than anything you can buy. Turns out there actually *is* such a thing as a free lunch!

There are other options for the vegetable stock that you can explore if you like. For example, roasting the vegetables coated with olive oil on a sheet pan in the oven at 350 degrees for an hour results in browned vegetables, and simmering these results in a darker, richer stock. This could work well with hearty soups such as the *zuppa di cipolle* (onion soup) or the *zuppa d'inverno* (winter soup), but I would not recommend it for the more delicate soups such as the *broccoli al limone* (broccoli with lemon) or *vellutata di spinaci e pistacchi* (cream of spinach and pistachio). The strength of the roasted vegetable stock could overpower the delicate flavors of these soups, but feel free to experiment. It is also possible to customize the vegetable stock based on the other ingredients in the soup, such as making a leek-based vegetable stock for the *vellutata di porri e patate* (cream of leek and potato soup). Why not try broccoli stock for the *broccoli al limone* (broccoli with lemon soup) for an additional layer of broccoli goodness? The possibilities are nearly limitless.

BREAD

"I don't want bread with this soup," said no one ever. There never was a soup, especially an Italian soup, that was not improved by the addition of bread. Grilled bread, toasted bread, garlic bread, and *crostini* (croutons) all have their place in various situations. There are two specific recipes in this book, *pappa al pomodoro* (tomato and bread soup) and *ribollita* (reboiled soup) that require bread within the recipe, but for the rest you can just plan to serve your soups with bread for dipping and digging the last bits of soup out of the bottom of the bowl. For those recipes that nearly demand to be served with bread, I have listed it in the ingredient list, for others it could be served if desired. My favorite breads for soup are *filone* and *stirato*, long, thin loaves similar to what the thieving French call baguettes, as well as *ciabatta*. Sliced, drizzled with olive oil, and toasted in the oven or grilled on a panini press, these or any rustic loaves work well. *Crostini* (croutons), diced bread mixed with olive oil, dried herbs, salt, and pepper, and baked at 350 degrees for 15 minutes, scattered across the top of the soup are also wonderful.

BEANS

Many of the recipes in this book contain beans or legumes of one sort or another. I have specified cooked beans and legumes in the ingredient lists for all except for lentils and fava beans (when these are used, full instructions are included for cooking them). I have included cooked beans in the ingredient lists so you can choose between cooking the beans yourself or using canned beans. When buying canned beans, I usually buy the low-salt versions and rinse away the liquid, although this is not mandatory. Canned beans are cheap (the only thing cheaper might be...dried beans) as well as evenly and perfectly cooked every time, and they have good flavor.

If you want to cook your own beans, by all means do so, and the cooking time can usually be halved by soaking the beans in water overnight. Then, simmer the beans, covered, in plenty of water with a garlic clove cut in half and a bay leaf (no salt as it can stop beans from becoming tender). The beans are done when they are tender, and the cooking time varies quite a bit based on the type and age of the dried beans.

GARNISHES

It is common among cookbook authors to provide suggestions and photographs of elaborately garnished dishes, and I must admit that I have succumbed to this temptation myself at times. I want you to make and enjoy the soups in this book, and if a nice photograph convinces you to try a recipe, so be it. However, the soups in this book are rustic soups, mostly country soups, sometimes developed from recipes in use for centuries. I seriously doubt that my Calabrian great-great-great-great-great grandparents were delicately placing cross-cut green onions in a circular pattern around the edge of a color-matched bowl of onion soup. The closest they probably came was to stir in a handful of chopped parsley just before ladling the soup into bowls. Home cooks in the modern era are no different, dinner parties and first dates notwithstanding. Therefore, I have tried to keep the garnishes simple in this book, providing some suggestions rather than detailed instructions, with the suggestions often coming from the photos rather than the recipes themselves.

Speaking of parsley, the Italians have a saying, *sei come il prezzemolo*, meaning "you're like parsley," with the implication being that you are everywhere, always underfoot like an overly dependent child. Such is the presence of parsley in Italian dishes including soups. So, when in doubt, stir in a handful of chopped parsley when the soup is finished to provide a wonderful color accent and fresh flavor.

In Southern Italy, *formaggio dei poveri* (the cheese of the poor) meant *pangrattato aromatico* (aromatic breadcrumbs). This was historically used instead of the expensive grating cheeses from the North, and the Southerners did not miss a thing. Fried in olive oil with salt, pepper, minced garlic, and parsley or other fresh or dried herbs for about 2 minutes at medium heat, these breadcrumbs make a wonderfully crunchy and flavorful addition to the *vellutate* (cream soups) in this book. Ultimately, as noted above, a half-submerged hunk of crusty bread is an Italian soup's best friend and the only garnish we usually need.

RECIPES AS SUGGESTIONS

Although it is impossible to write a proper cookbook without recipes, the soups in this book are not fixed and are not made the same way from town to town and region to region in Italy. The Italians have three separate phrases to communicate this idea. *A occhio* translates as "to the eye," meaning that you should add as much of a particular ingredient as looks right, rather than measuring things by the tablespoon, cup, liter, pound, or gram. Just eyeball it, as we would say in English. *Quanto basta* (often abbreviated as "qb" in Italian recipes) means "as much as is enough," a bit of circular logic that makes its point. Finally, *a piacere* means that you should add "a pleasing amount," which would be different for every cook. The Italians are trying to tell us something with this redundancy: make it the way you like it, not the way the recipe commands. The best Italian cooks value their own judgement over strict recipe instructions. In fact, for some of the recipes in this book (such as *zuppa del contadino*, farmer's soup), I was tempted to add simply quanto basta after every ingredient rather than specific amounts.

The point is that the Italians know well that different tastes require different ingredients and different amounts of those ingredients. Ask an Italian cook how much salt is needed for their famous soup and he or she will no doubt say "as much as it needs" or "until it tastes right" rather than "1½ tablespoons" or "7 grams." You prefer limes to lemons? Make broccoli with lime soup instead of broccoli with lemon soup. No marjoram in the house? Add thyme instead to the red lentil soup. The soups and recipes in this book are merely ideas to guide you, not rules to constrain you. If you learn how to make a good soffritto, if you are using delicious vegetable stock, and if your ingredients are fresh, it is hard to make a bad soup.

ORGANIZATION OF THE BOOK

Let's face it, although sometimes we are ready to roll up our sleeves, sharpen our knives, send the dog to bed and put on our chef's hats, other times (maybe most of the time) we just want a delicious and nutritious meal without too much fuss. Well, you have come to the right place. I have arranged the recipes in this book from easiest to most difficult, although even the most difficult are not terribly so. You might start by trying some of the recipes near the beginning of the book so that you can work on your soffritto and vegetable stock while still enjoying some amazing meals, and then delve deeper into the recipes toward the middle and back of the book when you are feeling a bit more adventurous.

Enjoy.

FACILISSIMO (VERY EASY)

ZUPPA DI POMODORI E FINOCCHI
(TOMATO AND FENNEL SOUP)

Adding plenty of fresh fennel and fennel seeds to a traditional Italian tomato soup recipe gives this dish a much-needed upgrade. Although wild fennel is often used in Italy, it is difficult to find, and luckily the mild anise flavor of any fennel gives this tomato soup an unexpected and lovely note. Adding crushed fennel seeds reinforces that flavor, and the basil added at the end further freshens up the soup. You can use fire roasted or San Marzano tomatoes for a flavor bump. Aromatic breadcrumbs (*pangrattato aromatico*) are a nice crunchy addition to this soup. Just blend a slice of bread, a peeled garlic clove, and a few leaves of basil in a food processor for a minute or two, then fry for a minute or so in a bit of olive oil on medium heat. Be careful when frying the breadcrumbs as they go from "is this even working?" to "what happened to this?" in a few seconds.

Ingredients (6 large servings)

3 tablespoons olive oil

1 onion, peeled and diced small

3 fennel bulbs, cleaned and diced small

1 tablespoon fennel seeds, crushed

3 garlic cloves, minced

2 cans (14 ounces each) diced tomatoes

3 cups vegetable stock

10 basil leaves, julienned

Salt and pepper to taste

Procedures

1. Make a golden soffritto in a soup pot by frying the onion, fennel, fennel seeds, and a pinch of salt in the olive oil on medium-low heat for 15 minutes, adding the garlic in the last minute.

2. Add the tomatoes and vegetable stock and simmer, covered, for 1 hour.

3. Stir in basil, taste, and add salt and pepper as desired.

CREMA DI CANNELLINI ALLA PAPRIKA
(CANNELLINI BEAN SOUP WITH PAPRIKA)

    The peppers used to make paprika are from the New World, but they quickly made their way across Europe. This spice was incorporated into recipes from Portugal to Italy and beyond. It is important to add the paprika to the oil when making the soffritto rather than later in the recipe because the aroma and flavors of the paprika will be unleashed only with the higher temperatures. You can't miss the unusual and enticing aroma of frying paprika.

Ingredients (6 large servings)

3 tablespoons olive oil
1 onion, peeled and diced small
1 carrot, peeled and diced small
Leaves from 1 sprig of rosemary
1 tablespoon paprika (preferably smoked)
2 potatoes (yellow or whichever you have), peeled and diced
3 cups cooked cannellini beans (or two 15-ounce cans, drained)
6 cups vegetable stock
Salt and pepper to taste
1 teaspoon thyme leaves

Procedures

1. Make a golden soffritto in a soup pot by frying the onion, carrot, rosemary, paprika, and a pinch of salt in the olive oil on medium-low heat for 10 minutes.

2. Add the potato, beans, and vegetable stock and simmer, covered, for 30 minutes.

3. Turn off the heat and set aside 1 cup of the soup; blend the remaining soup with an immersion blender until completely smooth and creamy (or process in a food processor) and then add back the reserved unblended soup.

4. Taste and add salt and pepper as desired.

5. Ladle into bowls and garnish with the thyme leaves and a bit more paprika.

ZUPPA DI PATATE, PORRI, E FUNGHI
(POTATO, LEEK, AND MUSHROOM SOUP)

An incredibly simple soup that lets the natural flavors of the leeks and mushrooms shine through, this is perfect for a cold winter day. The bit of citrus juice added at the end brightens up what could otherwise be an overly earthy soup. A nice garnish is *funghi trifolati*, or "mushrooms prepared as you would prepare truffles," which is to say fried in olive oil with garlic and parsley. Simply slice a few mushrooms and fry them in a tablespoon of olive oil at medium heat for 5 minutes or so until they begin to nicely brown, and then toss in some parsley and garlic and fry for another minute. If you do not have an immersion blender, you can blend the soup in a food processor, simply break up the potatoes with a potato masher, or even just whisk vigorously.

Ingredients (6 large servings)

3 tablespoons olive oil + 1 tablespoon for drizzling
3 leeks, white and light green parts only, peeled, sliced thinly, and rinsed well
2 potatoes (yellow or whichever you have), peeled and diced
4 cups diced mushrooms (porcini, cremini, or any non-dried mushrooms)
1 tablespoon thyme leaves
4 cups vegetable stock
Juice of ½ lemon or lime
Salt and pepper to taste

Procedures

1. Add the leeks, potatoes, mushrooms, thyme, and a pinch of salt to a soup pot with the 3 tablespoons of olive oil on medium-low heat.

2. Fry, stirring a few times, for 10 minutes until the mixture begins to dry.

3. Add the vegetable stock and simmer, covered, for 30 minutes.

4. Turn off the heat and blend soup with an immersion blender until thickened but with small pieces of vegetable remaining.

5. Add the lemon or lime juice, taste, and add salt and pepper as desired.

6. Ladle into bowls and drizzle with the reserved olive oil.

ZUPPA AUTUNNALE
(AUTUMN SOUP)

Buy an extra pumpkin or two when it is time to carve Jack-o-Lanterns for Halloween so that you can make this delectable soup or use butternut squash for a sweeter flavor. Filled with seasonal vegetables such as leeks, potatoes, and bitter greens, this soup marks the end of a gardener's time in the sun. The skins from the pumpkin or butternut squash can be more easily removed with a vegetable peeler (going a few layers deep) than with a knife, and removing one side to allow it to lay flat on your cutting board makes it easier to dice, as does a sharp knife.

Ingredients (6 large servings)

2 tablespoons olive oil

2 leeks, white and light green parts only, peeled, sliced thinly, and rinsed well

2 pounds peeled, cleaned, and diced pumpkin (or butternut squash)

1 cup chopped black kale, mustard greens, or other bitter green

4 cups vegetable stock

Leaves from 1 sprig of rosemary, roughly chopped

1 bay leaf

1½ cups cooked borlotti or pinto beans (or one 15-ounce can, drained)

Salt and pepper to taste

Procedures

1. Make a golden soffritto in a soup pot by frying the leeks and a pinch of salt in the olive oil on medium-low heat for 10 minutes.

2. Add the pumpkin, kale, vegetable stock, rosemary, and bay leaf and simmer, covered, for 20 minutes.

3. Add the beans and simmer for another 5 minutes.

4. Taste and add salt and pepper as desired.

5. Whoever gets the bay leaf kisses the cook.

MINESTRONE DI ORZO E LEGUMI
(BARLEY AND LEGUME SOUP)

Although there is a type of pasta called orzo, the orzo in this soup is barley, not pasta. This soup is often eaten in Trentino Alto Adige, a region so far north in Italy that most of it lies between Switzerland and Austria. Barley is one of the oldest cultivated crops in the world, and Italians love it so much they have even developed a coffee substitute made from roasted barley, *caffè d'orzo* (although the rationing of coffee during the Second World War also had something to do with this). As it cooks, the barley in this soup releases its starch, turning the thin vegetable stock base into a sumptuous broth.

Ingredients (6 large servings)

3 tablespoons olive oil

1 onion, peeled and diced small

1 carrot, peeled and diced small

1 celery stalk, diced small

2 tablespoons chopped fresh sage

2 garlic cloves, minced

7 cups vegetable stock

1½ cups cooked black beans (one 15-ounce can, drained)

1½ cups cooked cannellini beans (one 15-ounce can, drained)

1 cup pearled barley

Salt and pepper to taste

Procedures

1. Make a golden soffritto in a soup pot by frying the onion, carrot, celery, sage, and a pinch of salt in the olive oil on medium-low heat for 10 minutes, adding the garlic in the last minute.

2. Add the vegetable stock, beans, and pearled barley and simmer, covered, for 30 minutes or until the pearled barley is tender.

3. Taste and add salt and pepper as desired.

ZUPPA DI LENTICCHIE ROSSE
(RED LENTIL SOUP)

Simple, inexpensive, nutritious, and delicious, this soup is everything an Italian soup should be. It is reputed to be a *toccasana*, meaning a dish with healing properties of the, shall we say, somewhat magical variety? I would not doubt it for a minute. Maybe it is the marjoram, the forgotten herb, thyme's older, more sophisticated sister. You can reserve a few of the marjoram leaves and use as a garnish if you like, and do not scrimp on the crushed red pepper.

Ingredients (6 large servings)

3 tablespoons olive oil

1 onion, peeled and diced small

2 carrots, peeled and diced small

2 celery stalks, diced small

2 tablespoons fresh marjoram leaves (or 2 teaspoons dried)

1 teaspoon crushed red pepper

1 tablespoon tomato paste

2 garlic cloves, minced

3 cups dried red lentils

6 cups vegetable stock

1 bay leaf

Salt and pepper to taste

Procedures

1. Make a golden soffritto in a soup pot by frying the onion, carrot, celery, marjoram leaves, crushed red pepper, tomato paste, and a pinch of salt in the olive oil on medium-low heat for 10 minutes, adding the garlic in the last minute.

2. Add the lentils, vegetable stock, and bay leaf and simmer, covered, for 20 minutes.

3. Taste and add salt and pepper as desired.

ZUPPA DI CARCIOFI E FUNGHI
(ARTICHOKE AND MUSHROOM SOUP)

Although it would be a real treat to use fresh artichokes in this recipe, they are often not available and require additional work to process. Using canned or marinated artichokes or artichoke hearts works well and results in a soup with just the right amount of tanginess.

Ingredients (6 large servings)

3 tablespoons olive oil

2 garlic cloves, minced

2 cups prepared (canned or marinated) artichokes, drained

2 cups diced mushrooms (porcini, cremini, or any non-dried mushrooms)

4 potatoes (yellow or whichever you have), peeled and diced

4 cups vegetable stock

Salt and pepper to taste

2 tablespoons chopped parsley

Procedures

1. Add the garlic, artichokes, mushrooms, potatoes, and a pinch of salt to a soup pot with the olive oil on medium-low heat.

2. Fry for 10 minutes until the mixture begins to dry.

3. Add the vegetable stock and simmer, covered, for 30 minutes.

4. Taste, add salt and pepper as desired, and garnish with parsley.

VELLUTATA DI SPINACI E PISTACCHI
(SPINACH AND PISTACHIO SOUP)

This soup is delicious and refreshing at room temperature as well as hot, so after blending you can decide to bring it back to a simmer or serve as is. This is one of the few soups in this book that is best eaten the day it is completed (most of the others develop happily for a day or two in the refrigerator) because the fresh taste of the spinach and dill fades over time, and the spartan green color turns army green overnight.

Ingredients (6 large servings)

2 tablespoons olive oil

1 onion, peeled and diced small

1 pound baby spinach, washed

6 cups vegetable stock

3 ounces pistachios, roughly chopped (½ ounce reserved for garnish)

1 medium avocado, diced or sliced (half reserved for garnish)

¼ cup chopped dill

Juice of ½ lemon

Salt and pepper to taste

Procedures

1. Make a light soffritto in a soup pot by frying the onion with a pinch of salt in the olive oil on medium-low heat for 5 minutes.

2. Add the spinach, stir well, and cook for 2 minutes.

3. Turn off the heat, add the vegetable stock, pistachios, half of the avocado, the dill, and the lemon juice.

4. Blend the soup with an immersion blender until smooth and creamy (or process in a food processor) and reheat to just under a simmer (or less if serving at room temperature).

5. Taste and add salt and pepper as desired.

6. Ladle into bowls and garnish with slices or pieces of avocado and chopped pistachio.

VELLUTATA DI PORRI E PATATE
(CREAM OF LEEK AND POTATO SOUP)

If you love leeks, this is the recipe for you. The potatoes are there to produce a creamy texture and the thyme adds a nice accent, but this soup is all about the tangy sweetness of the leeks and the crunchiness of the crispy croutons (or is that the crispiness of the crunchy croutons?). Seasoned croutons can be purchased or made by dicing bread into crouton-sized pieces (shocking, I know), mixing the pieces with salt, pepper, and olive oil, and baking for 15 minutes at 350 degrees.

Ingredients (6 large servings)

3 tablespoons olive oil

4 leeks, white and light green parts only, peeled, sliced thinly, and rinsed well

4 potatoes (yellow or whichever you have), peeled and diced

6 cups vegetable stock

Salt and pepper to taste

1 teaspoon thyme leaves

1 cup seasoned croutons

Procedures

1. Make a golden soffritto in a soup pot by frying the leek and a pinch of salt in the olive oil on medium-low heat for 10 minutes.

2. Add the potatoes and vegetable stock and simmer, covered, for 25 minutes.

3. Turn off the heat and blend the soup with an immersion blender until completely smooth and creamy (or process in a food processor).

4. Taste and add salt and pepper as desired.

5. Ladle into bowls and garnish with the thyme leaves and croutons.

PAPPA AL POMODORO
(TOMATO AND BREAD SOUP)

This is a great soup to make when you find yourself with some bread on its last legs, since stale or dry bread is best (but not mandatory) for absorbing the juices of the tomato. In fact, it is not entirely accurate to call *pappa al pomodoro* a soup—it should be thick and could easily be eaten with a fork. I unknowingly made a simple version of this soup many times as a child as I was frequently too impatient to cook spaghetti and opted to simply pour tomato sauce over bread. The first step is to make a thin tomato sauce, and then the bread is added to soak up the extra liquid. I like to use fire-roasted canned tomatoes or, if you feel like splurging, try certified San Marzano tomatoes from Italy.

Ingredients (6 large servings)

3 tablespoons olive oil
1 onion, peeled and diced small
1 carrot, peeled and diced small
2 celery stalks, diced small
1 tablespoon dried Italian herbs
½ teaspoon crushed red pepper
2 garlic cloves, minced
2 cups vegetable stock
2 cans (14 ounces each) diced tomatoes
½ loaf bread (approximately 10 ounces), cut or torn into bite-sized chunks
10 basil leaves, roughly chopped or torn
Salt and pepper to taste

Procedures

1. Make a golden soffritto in a soup pot by frying the onion, carrot, celery, dried herbs, crushed red pepper, and a pinch of salt in the olive oil on medium-low heat for 10 minutes, adding the garlic in the last minute.

2. Add the stock and tomatoes and simmer, covered, for 45 minutes.

3. Add the bread chunks and simmer for 15 minutes, stirring often. If the "soup" is sticking to the bottom of the pot, add a bit more stock or water.

4. Stir in the basil, turn off the heat, and let the soup cool to just above room temperature.

5. Taste and add salt and pepper as desired.

CREMA DI PORCINI E CASTAGNE
(MUSHROOM AND CHESTNUT SOUP)

This soup is a glorious combination of earthy flavors and colors. I use snack versions of whole roasted and peeled chestnuts in this recipe, available online or at specialty grocers (usually in 5- or 6-ounce pouches, so you'd need three such pouches for this soup). The slightly sweet chestnuts are the perfect accompaniment to the savory vegetables and mushrooms.

Ingredients (6 large servings)

4 tablespoons olive oil + 1 tablespoon for drizzling
1 onion, peeled and diced small
1 carrot, peeled and diced small
1 celery stalk, diced small
4 cups diced mushrooms (porcini, cremini, or any non-dried mushrooms)
2 garlic cloves, minced
1 pound chestnuts, roughly chopped (reserve 1 ounce for garnish)
4 cups vegetable stock
Salt and pepper to taste

Procedures

1. Make a golden soffritto in a soup pot by frying the onion, carrot, celery, mushrooms, and a pinch of salt in the olive oil on medium-low heat for 10 minutes, adding the garlic in the last minute.

2. Add the chestnuts and vegetable stock and simmer, covered, for 30 minutes.

3. Turn off the heat and blend the soup with an immersion blender until smooth and creamy (or process in a food processor).

4. Taste and add salt and pepper as desired.

5. Ladle into bowls and garnish with reserved chopped chestnuts and a drizzle of olive oil.

ZUPPA DI CIPOLLE (ONION SOUP)

For most of the recipes in this book, any type of yellow onion will do, but in this recipe the onions play such a central role that I prefer to use sweet yellow onions (Vidalia or Walla Walla or similar). In addition, the initial step of this recipe involves caramelizing the onions for an extended period of time and the higher level of sugar in sweet onions helps in this process. *The caramelization of the onions is the central technique of this soup.* It takes some time and should be done at a relatively low temperature; we do not want frantically frying onions here, but onions relaxing in a gently bubbling jacuzzi of olive oil. Brown is delicious, dark brown is better, but black is burned—it is a fine line, but one worth walking. As the caramelization process nears its end, you may hear the onions whispering things like "are we *still* cooking?" or "they're absolutely *mad*!" but don't let that stop you. Seasoned croutons can be purchased or made by dicing bread into crouton-sized pieces, mixing the pieces with salt, pepper, and olive oil, and baking for 15 minutes at 350 degrees.

Ingredients (6 large servings)

4 tablespoons olive oil
4 sweet onions, peeled and diced small
8 cups vegetable stock
1 bay leaf
Leaves from 1 sprig of rosemary, roughly chopped
2 potatoes (yellow or whichever you have), peeled and diced
Salt and pepper to taste
3 green onions or chives, chopped
2 cups seasoned croutons

Procedures

1. Add the onion with a pinch of salt to a soup pot with the olive oil on medium-low heat. Stir every few minutes for 30 minutes, scraping up the browning bottom of the pot as the caramelized sugars form. It is fine to add a tablespoon of water when you stir to help in scraping the bottom if it is too sticky.

2. Reduce the heat to low and continue to fry and stir and scrape every few minutes for an additional 10 minutes. This is where we go from *good enough* to *spectacular*.

3. Add the vegetable stock, bay leaf, rosemary, and potatoes and simmer, covered, for 20 minutes, or until the potatoes are fully cooked.

4. At this point you can briefly mash the soup with a potato masher or use an immersion blender for 10 seconds (remove the bay leaf first!). It is nice to develop a thick texture to the soup while retaining chunks of potato and onion, but this is not necessary—it can be left as is, partially pureed, or completely pureed (again, minus the bay leaf; did I mention you need to remove the bay leaf?).

5. Taste and add salt and pepper as desired.

6. Ladle into bowls and garnish with chopped green onions or chives and croutons.

FACILE (EASY)

ZUPPA DI PISELLI SPEZZATI
(SPLIT PEA SOUP)

    Although split peas are not as common as other types of legumes, they make for a nice change and this soup is perfect for a cold winter day. You can cut the cooking time after adding the split peas in half by soaking them in water overnight as you would with other beans. On the other hand, soaking the split peas overnight while maintaining the longer cooking time allows the split peas and potatoes to begin to dissolve, resulting in a wonderful creamy version of this soup. I would venture to say that it is impossible, or nearly so, to overcook this soup.

Ingredients (6 large servings)

3 tablespoons olive oil

1 onion, peeled and diced small

3 carrots, peeled and diced small

1 tablespoon dried Italian herbs

1 teaspoon crushed red pepper

2 garlic cloves, minced

2 cups dried split peas

6 cups vegetable stock

3 potatoes (yellow or whichever you have), peeled and diced

1 bay leaf

Salt and pepper to taste

Procedures

1. Make a golden soffritto in a soup pot by frying the onion, carrot, Italian herbs, crushed red pepper, and a pinch of salt in the olive oil on medium-low heat for 10 minutes, adding the garlic in the last minute.

2. Add the split peas and stir well.

3. Add the vegetable stock, potatoes, and bay leaf and simmer, covered, for 1½ hours or until the split peas are soft.

4. Taste and add salt and pepper as desired.

ZUPPA DI ZUCCA E CECI
(PUMPKIN AND CHICKPEA SOUP)

The glorious color of this soup is reason enough to make it, but the sweet flavor of the pumpkin or squash combined with the earthy greens is the main event. It would be a shame not to toast the pumpkin seeds (baked on a piece of tinfoil at 350 degrees for 20-25 minutes, mixing with a fork a few times to ensure even toasting, and finishing them up with a pinch of salt). Serve the pumpkin seeds along with the soup or greedily eat them yourself while everyone else is watching the game before dinner.

Ingredients (6 large servings)

- 2 tablespoons olive oil
- 1 onion, peeled and diced small
- 6 cups vegetable stock
- 1½ pounds peeled, cleaned, and diced pumpkin (or butternut squash)
- 2 bay leaves
- 10 juniper berries (precisely!)
- 3 cups cooked chickpeas (two 15-ounce cans, drained)
- 1 cup chopped black kale, mustard greens, or other bitter green
- Salt and pepper to taste

Procedures

1. Make a light soffritto in a soup pot by frying the onion and a pinch of salt in the olive oil on medium-low heat for 5 minutes.

2. Add the vegetable stock, pumpkin, bay leaves, and juniper berries and simmer, covered, for 30 minutes.

3. Remove the bay leaves and each of the juniper berries (they'll usually be floating on top, and otherwise are easy to see). Turn off the heat and blend the soup with an immersion blender until completely smooth and creamy (or process in a food processor).

4. After blending, add the chickpeas and bitter greens and simmer, covered, for an additional 10 minutes.

5. Taste and add salt and pepper as desired.

ZUPPA DI FAGIOLI BIANCHI
(TUSCAN WHITE BEAN SOUP)

Beans are beloved in all parts of Italy, but people in the region of Tuscany aren't called *mangiafagioli* (bean eaters) for nothing. The favorite type of bean among Tuscans is the white cannellini bean, known for its high protein content and very creamy texture. This soup is a perfect expression of the historic use of beans instead of meat out of necessity and poverty to produce phenomenal yet accidentally vegan soups.

Ingredients (6 large servings)

3 tablespoons olive oil
2 carrots, peeled and diced small
Leaves from 1 sprig of rosemary
5 garlic cloves, minced
4½ cups vegetable stock
4½ cups cooked cannellini beans (or three 15-ounce cans, drained)
1 cup chopped spinach, black kale, mustard greens, or other bitter green
Juice of ½ lemon
Salt and pepper to taste
6 slices rustic bread, toasted or grilled
¼ cup chopped parsley

Procedures

1. Make a golden soffritto in a soup pot by frying the carrot, rosemary, and a pinch of salt in the olive oil on medium-low heat for 10 minutes, adding the garlic in the last minute.

2. Add the vegetable stock, beans, and spinach or bitter greens and simmer, covered, for 15 minutes.

3. Mash the soup with a fork or potato masher, gently (it's hot!) but enough to create a creamy broth.

4. Add the lemon juice, taste, and add salt and pepper as desired.

5. Ladle into bowls, add a slice of bread, and top with chopped parsley.

PASTA E CECI (PASTA AND CHICKPEA SOUP)

This Roman meal can be a soup or a pasta dish, although the best version is somewhere in between. Garbanzo beans, also known as chickpeas, or, in Italian, *ceci*, are the dominant flavor in this dish although it is a delicate flavor. Canned chickpeas often have a creamier texture and sweeter flavor than those made from dried chickpeas, and I prefer the former in this dish.

Ingredients (6 large servings)

3 tablespoons olive oil + 1 tablespoon for drizzling
1 onion, peeled and diced small
1 carrot, peeled and diced small
2 celery stalks, diced small
1 tablespoon dried Italian herbs
Leaves from 1 sprig of rosemary, roughly chopped
½ teaspoon crushed red pepper
3 garlic cloves, minced
7 cups vegetable stock
1½ cups cooked chickpeas (one 15-ounce can, drained)
2 Roma tomatoes, diced (or half of one 14-ounce can)
4 ounces small dried pasta (such as ditalini, avemarie, or orzo)
Salt and pepper to taste

Procedures

1. Make a golden soffritto in a soup pot by frying the onion, carrot, celery, dried herbs, rosemary, crushed red pepper, and a pinch of salt in the olive oil on medium-low heat for 10 minutes, adding the garlic in the last minute.

2. Add the vegetable stock, chickpeas, and tomato and simmer, covered, for 30 minutes.

3. Add the dry pasta approximately 12 minutes before service and continue simmering.

4. Taste and add salt and pepper as desired.

5. Ladle into bowls and drizzle each bowl with olive oil.

MINESTRA DI LENTICCHIE E SCAROLA
(LENTIL AND ESCAROLE SOUP)

They love their lentils in Abruzzo and Umbria in Central Italy, especially on New Year's Eve when dishes like this soup are prepared. Bitter greens such as *scarola* (escarole), *cavolo nero* (kale) or *bietole* (Swiss chard) live in Italian gardens well into winter and provide a fresh (if slightly bitter and earthy) taste to this soup made primarily from lentils and dry pasta.

Ingredients (6 large servings)

- 3 tablespoons olive oil
- 1 onion, peeled and diced small
- 1 carrot, peeled and diced small
- 2 celery stalks, diced small
- 2 garlic cloves, minced
- 7 cups vegetable stock
- 2 cups dried lentils
- 4 Roma tomatoes, diced (or one 14-ounce can)
- 1 bay leaf
- 4 ounces small dried pasta (ditalini, avemarie, or orzo)
- 2 cups chopped escarole, spinach, or other bitter green
- Salt and pepper to taste

Procedures

1. Make a golden soffritto in a soup pot by frying the onion, carrot, celery, and a pinch of salt in the olive oil on medium-low heat for 10 minutes, adding the garlic in the last minute.

2. Add the vegetable stock, lentils, tomatoes, and bay leaf and simmer, covered, for 35 minutes. Check that the lentils are fully cooked or nearly so.

3. Add the pasta and escarole and cook for an additional 12 minutes.

4. Taste and add salt and pepper as desired.

CREMA DI ASPARAGI E PATATE
(CREAM OF ASPARAGUS AND POTATO SOUP)

    The unusual combination of asparagus and potatoes is brought to life with the addition of the citrus juice in this recipe. If you are trying to impress your dinner guests or significant other (and who isn't?), instead of adding the asparagus tips along with the other pieces of asparagus to the soup before blending, boil them separately in salted water for 3 minutes (much longer and they will lose their color) and use as a garnish. Seasoned croutons can be purchased or made by dicing bread into crouton-sized pieces, mixing the pieces with salt, pepper, and olive oil, and baking for 15 minutes at 350 degrees.

Ingredients (6 large servings)

3 tablespoons olive oil

4 leeks, white and light green parts only, peeled, sliced thinly, and rinsed well

8 cups vegetable stock

40 asparagus spears, top half only, washed and cut into half-inch pieces

2 potatoes (yellow or whichever you have), peeled and diced

Juice of ½ lemon or lime

1 teaspoon nutmeg (fresh ground if possible)

Salt and pepper to taste

1 cup seasoned croutons

Procedures

1. Make a golden soffritto in a soup pot by frying the leeks and a pinch of salt in the olive oil on medium-low heat for 10 minutes.

2. Add the vegetable stock, asparagus pieces, and potato and simmer, covered, for 30 minutes.

3. Add the lemon or lime juice and nutmeg, turn off the heat, and blend the soup with an immersion blender until smooth and creamy (or process in a food processor).

4. Taste and add salt and pepper as desired.

5. Ladle into bowls and garnish with asparagus tips (if using) and croutons.

CREMA DI BROCCOLI AL LIMONE
(CREAM OF BROCCOLI SOUP)

To have bright green, fresh looking soup, it is necessary to cook the potatoes and broccoli separately. An extra step, yes, and if you are color blind or unconcerned, don't bother, but for the rest of us the effort will be worth it. It is also helpful to cut the broccoli into smaller pieces than you typically might so that it will cook faster (time is your enemy when trying to keep broccoli bright green during the cooking process). This light soup is perfect for a summer lunch.

Ingredients (6 large servings)

2 tablespoons olive oil
1 onion, peeled and diced small
2 potatoes (yellow or whichever you have), peeled and diced
6 cups vegetable stock
1½ pounds broccoli, stalks removed and cut into small florets and pieces
Juice of ½ lemon
1 teaspoon cumin
Salt and pepper to taste

Procedures

1. Bring 4 quarts of water to a boil in a large pot and add 1 tablespoon of salt.
2. Make a light soffritto in a separate soup pot by frying the onion and a pinch of salt in the olive oil on medium-low heat for 5 minutes.
3. Add the potato and stock to the soup pot and simmer, covered, for 20 minutes until the potato flesh is soft.
4. While the potato is cooking, add the broccoli to the boiling, salted water pot and boil for 5 minutes.
5. Strain the broccoli and rinse under cold water to stop the cooking (or immerse in ice water). Reserve a few nice pieces of broccoli for garnish.
6. When the potatoes are cooked, add the non-garnish broccoli, turn off the heat, and blend the soup with an immersion blender until completely smooth and creamy (or process in a food processor).
7. Reheat a bit if necessary, but do not simmer again.
8. Add the lemon juice and cumin, taste, and add salt and pepper as desired.
9. If necessary, add a bit of water for a soupier consistency.
10. Ladle into bowls and garnish with the reserved broccoli.

BORDATINO PISANO (ON BOARD SOUP)

    The maritime republics were a group of city-states in Italy from the tenth and fifteenth centuries that built military and economic power through trade in Mediterranean waters. The most powerful were Venice, Genoa, Amalfi, and the namesake for this soup, Pisa. This soup was served on board the ships as they traversed the open sea, with the phrase *a bordo* meaning "on board." One of the ingredients for this soup is the water used in cooking the beans (nothing was wasted on these voyages), and therefore we will start with dried beans soaked overnight for this recipe. Cannellini beans or white kidney beans can be used (but not lima beans, please I beg you not lima beans!).

Ingredients (6 large servings)

3 cups dried white beans, soaked overnight at room temperature
2 garlic cloves, crushed and peeled
1 bay leaf
3 tablespoons olive oil
1 onion, peeled and diced small
1 carrot, peeled and diced small
1 celery stalk, diced small
2 tablespoons chopped parsley
2 tablespoons tomato paste
2 cups finely chopped black kale, mustard greens, or other bitter green
1 cup cornmeal (yellow or white, medium or coarse)
Salt and pepper to taste

Procedures

1. Rinse the soaked beans and add to a pot covered by 2 inches of water with the crushed garlic cloves and the bay leaf. Cover and simmer for 1 hour until the beans are soft (possibly more depending on the age of the beans). Do not drain the water.

2. When the beans are cooked, make a golden (if reddish) soffritto in a separate soup pot by frying the onion, carrot, celery, chopped parsley, tomato paste, and a pinch of salt in the olive oil on medium-low heat for 10 minutes.

3. Remove the bay leaf and crushed garlic cloves from the bean water. Strain the beans, reserving the water.

4. Add half of the cooked beans and 3 cups of the bean cooking liquid to the soup pot with the soffritto and blend the soup with an immersion blender for 30 seconds (or process in a food processor).

5. Add the remaining beans, the bitter greens, and 3 more cups of the bean cooking liquid to the pot (if you run out, use water). Slowly sprinkle in the cornmeal while stirring vigorously (to avoid clumping) and simmer, covered, for 20 minutes. Stir frequently to ensure that the thick soup does not stick.

6. Taste and add salt and pepper as desired.

ZUPPA DEL CONTADINO
(FARMER'S SOUP)

    Be flexible with this thick and hearty soup—it is prepared differently in every farmer's kitchen from Tuscany to Calabria. The mainstays are the aromatic vegetables in the soffritto, assorted beans, and tomatoes. In this soup the aromatic vegetables of onion, carrot, and celery need not be diced small as in the typical soffritto because large chunks are desirable in the finished product.

Ingredients (6 large servings)

3 tablespoons olive oil
1 onion, peeled and diced
1 carrot, peeled and diced
1 celery stalk, diced
½ teaspoon crushed red pepper
Leaves from 1 sprig of rosemary, roughly chopped
2 garlic cloves, minced
2 tablespoons tomato paste
½ cup dried lentils
4 Roma tomatoes, diced (or one 14-ounce can)
4 cups vegetable stock
1½ cups cooked borlotti or pinto beans (or one 15-ounce can, drained)
1½ cups cooked chickpeas (or one 15-ounce can, drained)
1 potato (yellow or whichever you have), peeled and diced
Salt and pepper to taste

Procedures

1. Make a golden soffritto in a soup pot by frying the onion, carrot, celery, crushed red pepper, rosemary leaves, and a pinch of salt in the olive oil on medium-low heat for 10 minutes, adding the garlic and tomato paste in the last minute.

2. Add the lentils, tomatoes, and vegetable stock and simmer, covered, for 30 minutes.

3. Add the beans, chickpeas, and potato and simmer, covered, for an additional 30 minutes.

4. Taste and add salt and pepper as desired.

MACCÚ DI SAN GIUSEPPE
(SAINT JOSEPH'S SOUP)

The perfect accidentally vegan soup, this fava bean masterpiece is traditionally made for *La Festa di San Giuseppe* (The Festival of Saint Joseph) on March 19 during Lent, and so meat is not served in Sicily. Fava beans are considered good luck in Sicily, and some people even carry a dried bean in their pocket when extra luck is needed. Aromatic breadcrumbs (*pangrattato aromatico*) can be served on top and symbolize the sawdust from the Saint's carpentry work. Simply blend a slice of bread, a garlic clove, and some fresh herbs in a food processor for a minute or two, then fry for a minute or so in a bit of olive oil on medium heat.

Ingredients (6 large servings)

3 tablespoons olive oil
1 onion, peeled and diced small
2 fennel bulbs, cleaned and diced
½ teaspoon crushed red pepper
2 tablespoons minced sun-dried tomatoes
1½ cups (8 ounces) dried fava beans, soaked overnight at room temperature or for 2 days in the refrigerator, skins removed after soaking
6 cups vegetable stock
1 cup dried lentils
1½ cups cooked chickpeas (or one 15-ounce can, drained)
1½ cups cooked kidney beans (or one 15-ounce can, drained)
1 cup chopped black kale, mustard greens, or other bitter green
Salt and pepper to taste

Procedures

1. Make a golden soffritto in a soup pot by frying the onion, fennel, crushed red pepper, sun dried tomatoes, and a pinch of salt in the olive oil on medium-low heat for 10 minutes.

2. Add the soaked and peeled fava beans and the vegetable stock and simmer, covered, for 40 minutes.

3. Add the lentils and simmer, covered, for an additional 30 minutes.

4. Add the chickpeas, kidney beans, and bitter greens and simmer for another 5 minutes.

5. Taste and add salt and pepper as desired.

ZUPPA DI ZUCCA E CASTAGNE
(PUMPKIN AND CHESTNUT SOUP)

For this recipe, using prepared chestnuts is fine (although if it is Christmas season and you are already planning to roast chestnuts on an open fire...). You can find prepared chestnuts in specialty shops or online. I use the snack versions of whole roasted and peeled chestnuts available at several popular online shopping websites. You will need a lot, and they are not cheap, so this is a special occasion soup perfect for holiday get togethers. It is unusual to find an entirely new flavor combination, but this soup delivers.

Ingredients (6 large servings)

3 tablespoons olive oil
2 large shallots, peeled and diced small
1 tablespoon chopped rosemary or sage or both
2 garlic cloves, minced
1½ pounds peeled and diced pumpkin (or butternut squash)
6 cups vegetable stock
8 ounces chestnuts, roughly chopped (reserve 1 ounce for garnish)
1 teaspoon nutmeg (fresh ground if possible)
1 teaspoon turmeric
Salt and pepper to taste

Procedures

1. Make a golden soffritto in a soup pot by frying the shallots, fresh herbs, and a pinch of salt in the olive oil on medium-low heat for 10 minutes, adding the garlic in the last minute.

2. Add the prepared pumpkin and vegetable stock and simmer, covered, for 30 minutes until the pumpkin flesh is soft.

3. Add the chestnuts and blend the soup with an immersion blender until completely smooth and creamy (or process in a food processor).

4. Add the nutmeg and turmeric, taste, and add salt and pepper as desired.

5. Ladle into bowls and roughly chop the reserved chestnuts for garnish.

ZUPPA DI LEGUMI E ERBE AROMATICHE
(LEGUME AND HERB SOUP)

I would not use dried herbs in this recipe except in an emergency (admittedly, soup emergencies are common in my kitchen) because the sweeter flavor and stronger aroma of fresh herbs are central to this soup. I have specified rosemary, sage, and marjoram, but you could also add thyme, tarragon, oregano, or dill, or all of the above; the more the better.

Ingredients (6 large servings)

- 3 tablespoons olive oil
- 1 onion, peeled and diced small
- 1 carrot, peeled and diced small
- 1 celery stalk, diced small
- Leaves from 1 rosemary spring, roughly chopped
- 5 sage leaves, roughly chopped
- 1 tablespoon marjoram leaves (or 1 teaspoon dried)
- 1 bay leaf
- 1 cup dried lentils
- 2 cups chopped black kale, mustard greens, or other bitter green
- 6 cups vegetable stock
- 1½ cups cooked chickpeas (or one 15-ounce can, drained)
- Salt and pepper to taste

Procedures

1. Make a golden soffritto in a soup pot by frying the onion, carrot, celery, fresh herbs, and a pinch of salt in the olive oil on medium-low heat for 10 minutes.

2. Add the bay leaf, lentils, bitter greens, and vegetable stock and simmer, covered, for 40 minutes until the lentils are fully cooked.

3. Add the chickpeas and simmer for another 5 minutes.

4. Taste and add salt and pepper as desired.

SBROSCIA (TABLE SCRAP SOUP)

In case you think that "table scrap soup" is an unappetizing name, you'd reconsider if you realized that the other popular translation for the name of this soup in the Tuscan dialect would be something like "the sloshy, icy mess that accumulates on the ground as people walk through melting snow." But, in a good way. What makes this soup resemble the slushy end of winter is overcooking the pumpkin until the clean edges of each piece begin to dissolve and thicken the soup.

Ingredients (6 large servings)

- 3 tablespoons olive oil
- 1 onion, peeled and diced small
- 1 carrot, peeled and diced small
- 1 celery stalk, diced small
- 1 tablespoon fresh marjoram leaves (or 1 teaspoon dried)
- 5 sage leaves, roughly chopped
- 2 garlic cloves, minced
- 1 pound peeled and diced pumpkin (or butternut squash)
- 6 cups vegetable stock
- 1½ cups cooked kidney beans (or one 15-ounce can, drained)
- 2 tablespoons chopped parsley
- Salt and pepper to taste

Procedures

1. Make a golden soffritto in a soup pot by frying the onion, carrot, celery, marjoram, sage, and a pinch of salt in the olive oil on medium-low heat for 10 minutes, adding the garlic in the last minute.

2. Add the pumpkin and vegetable stock and simmer, covered, for 40 minutes until the pumpkin is beyond fully cooked.

3. Add the beans and simmer for an additional 5 minutes.

4. Stir in the chopped parsley, taste, and add salt and pepper as desired.

ZUPPA D'INVERNO (WINTER SOUP)

What could be better on a cold winter's day than a hot bowl of delicious soup? That's right, nothing could be better. This winter recipe takes advantage of the cabbage and bitter greens that stay fresh in the garden into winter to produce a hearty soup fit for a main course.

Ingredients (6 large servings)

4 tablespoons olive oil
2 leeks, white and light green parts only, peeled, sliced thinly, and rinsed well
2 carrots, peeled and diced small
2 celery stalks, diced small
2 garlic cloves, minced
2 Roma tomatoes, diced (or half of one 14-ounce can)
1 cup chopped cabbage
1 cup chopped black kale, mustard greens, or other bitter green
6 cups vegetable stock
1½ cups cooked borlotti or pinto beans (or one 15-ounce can, drained)
1½ cups cooked cannellini beans (or one 15-ounce can, drained)
Salt and pepper to taste
2 tablespoons chopped parsley

Procedures

1. Make a golden soffritto in a soup pot by frying the leek, carrot, celery, and a pinch of salt in the olive oil on medium-low heat for 10 minutes, adding the garlic in the last minute.

2. Add the tomatoes, cabbage, bitter greens, and vegetable stock and simmer, covered, for 30 minutes.

3. Add the beans and simmer for another 5 minutes.

4. Taste and add salt and pepper as desired.

5. Ladle into bowls and garnish with chopped parsley.

UN PO' PIÚ DIFFICILE
(A BIT MORE DIFFICULT)

MACCÚ (FAVA BEAN SOUP)

Pronounced *mah-coo,* this Sicilian soup packs a protein punch like no other in this book. Leftover *maccú* will firm up as it cools in the refrigerator and can be spread on top of toasty bread the next day (when you can call it fava puree and add red onion on top). If you can find canned fava beans, great, you will need 6 cups of cooked beans (four 15-ounce cans), but I usually can't. Therefore, for this recipe you will likely need to buy dried fava beans and prepare them prior to making the soup. Removing the skins from the fava beans after soaking overnight is fun—you grab the bean in the thumb and forefinger of both hands and roll the bean out of its skin, like unwrapping a hundred little Christmas presents.

INGREDIENTS (6 LARGE SERVINGS PLUS A BIT FOR SPREADING ON BREAD THE NEXT DAY)

3 tablespoons olive oil + 1 tablespoon for drizzling
2 fennel bulbs, cleaned and diced (save some fronds for garnish)
1 carrot, peeled and diced small
1 tablespoon fennel seeds (crushed in a mortar and pestle if you like)
½ teaspoon crushed red pepper
4 garlic cloves, minced
6 cups vegetable stock
3 cups (1 pound) of dried fava beans, soaked overnight at room temperature or for 2 days in the refrigerator, skins removed after soaking
Salt and pepper to taste
6 (or more) slices of rustic bread, grilled or toasted

PROCEDURES

1. Make a golden soffritto in a soup pot by frying the fennel, carrot, fennel seeds, crushed red pepper, and a pinch of salt in the olive oil on medium-low heat for 10 minutes, adding the garlic in the last minute.

2. Add the vegetable stock and the soaked and peeled fava beans and simmer, covered, for 1½ hours.

3. When a few test beans are soft, whisk the soup vigorously for at least a minute to break up the cooked beans so that the liquid thickens.

4. Taste and add salt and pepper as desired.

5. Place soup in bowls, drizzle a bit of extra-virgin olive oil in each bowl, garnish with chopped fennel fronds (no stems), and serve with a piece of bread. Or two. Three also works.

CIAMBOTTA (VEGETABLE STEW)

Call it *ciambotta*, *giambotta*, *ciambrotta*, *ciammotta*, *cianfotta*, or *ciabotta* (welcome to the wonderful world of Italian regional dialects), this thick vegetable stew is a favorite during the summer across Southern Italy. In addition to making research on this stew difficult, the variety of names and subsequent ingredient lists underscores the diversity of Italian cuisine, even within a particular dish. The vegetables used in the soffritto (onion and celery) do not need to be finely diced in this case because a chunky consistency is desired. This rich, robust vegetable stew gets a lift with the addition of the fresh herb *pestata* as a garnish. This soup is intensely flavored so plenty of bread should be served.

Ingredients (6 large servings)

3 tablespoons olive oil
1 onion, peeled and diced
1 celery stalk, diced
Leaves from 1 sprig of rosemary, roughly chopped
2 garlic cloves, crushed and peeled
2 tablespoons tomato paste
1 eggplant (skin on), diced
1 zucchini (skin on), diced
2 potatoes (yellow or whichever you have), peeled and diced
2 cans (14 ounces each) crushed or diced tomatoes with their juice
Salt and pepper to taste
12 slices of rustic bread, grilled or toasted

Pestata ingredients

2 tablespoons minced basil leaves
1 garlic clove, minced
½ teaspoon crushed red pepper
1 tablespoon olive oil

Procedures

1. Make a golden soffritto in a soup pot by frying the onion, celery, rosemary leaves, and a pinch of salt to the olive oil on medium-low heat for 10 minutes, adding the garlic and tomato paste in the last minute.

2. Add the eggplant, zucchini, and potato and fry for 5 minutes.

3. Add the tomatoes along with their juice and simmer, covered, for 30 minutes, stirring often. A bit of water can be added if the soup begins to look dry.

4. While the vegetables are simmering, make the pestata by adding the basil, garlic, and crushed red pepper to the olive oil in a frying pan on medium heat for 2 minutes.

5. Remove the vegetables from the stove and let cool to just above room temperature.

6. Taste the soup, add salt and pepper as desired, then spoon into bowls and top with a bit of pestata. Serve with plenty of bread.

RIBOLLITA (REBOILED SOUP)

Ribollita means "reboiled," and this Tuscan soup can be made and remade over several days. The version presented below is for Day 1. Before you put the leftovers in the refrigerator, layer the soup with bread. On Day 2, reheating the soup and bread mixture (i.e. reboiling) gives a thicker result that is more like a side dish than a soup. On Day 3, things get interesting as the "soup" at this point is nearly solid and can be formed into patties and fried in olive oil. Are you kidding me? The tough part is having any left on the third day, so you might want to make extra.

Ingredients (6 large servings)

3 tablespoons olive oil
1 onion, peeled and diced small
1 carrot, peeled and diced small
2 celery stalks, diced small
1 tablespoon dried Italian herbs
½ teaspoon crushed red pepper
3 garlic cloves, minced
6 cups vegetable stock
1 zucchini, diced
2 potatoes (yellow or whichever you have), peeled and diced
2 cups chopped black kale, mustard greens, or other bitter green
3 cups cooked cannellini beans (or two 15-ounce cans, drained)
6 thick slices rustic bread
Salt and pepper to taste

Procedures

1. Make a golden soffritto in a soup pot by frying the onion, carrot, celery, dried herbs, crushed red pepper, and a pinch of salt in the olive oil on medium-low heat for 10 minutes, adding the garlic in the last minute.

2. Add the vegetable stock, zucchini, potato, and kale and simmer, covered, for 20 minutes or until the potato is cooked.

3. Add the beans and simmer for an additional 5 minutes.

4. Taste and add salt and pepper as desired.

5. Place a slice of bread in the bottom of each bowl and ladle the soup over the top.

CREMA DI FAVE E ASPARAGI
(CREAM OF FAVA AND ASPARAGUS SOUP)

Wild asparagus (*asparagi selvatici*) is found throughout North America and Europe. Wild asparagus often has a stronger flavor than the store-bought variety, so if you can find it piercing the melting snow in your local woods (often around mid-April but this varies greatly by location), use it. Because canned fava beans are difficult to find, this recipe calls for dried fava beans, soaked for 24 hours before starting the soup, and then peeled. Don't forget that fava beans love bread as much as we love fava beans!

Ingredients (6 large servings)

3 tablespoons olive oil
1 onion, peeled and diced small
2 carrots, peeled and diced small
1 celery stalk, diced small
Leaves from 1 sprig of rosemary, roughly chopped
3 cups dried fava beans, soaked for 24 hours at room temperature or for 2 days in the refrigerator, skins removed after soaking
6 cups vegetable stock
40 asparagus spears, top half only, washed and cut into half-inch pieces
Salt and pepper to taste
6 slices of toasted or grilled bread

Procedures

1. Make a golden soffritto in a soup pot by frying the onion, carrot, celery, rosemary, and a pinch of salt in the olive oil on medium-low heat for 10 minutes.

2. Add the soaked and peeled fava beans and vegetable stock and simmer, covered, for 1½ hours.

3. Add a teaspoon of salt to a pot of boiling water and add the asparagus pieces for 2 minutes, drain, and set aside.

4. Blend the soup with an immersion blender for 30 seconds (or process in a food processor), and then stir in the asparagus pieces.

5. Taste, add salt and pepper as desired, and add a piece of bread to each bowl when serving.

Printed in Great Britain
by Amazon